SCOUBIDOU

FUN TIME

Yoarra

CONTENTS:

Colofon
© 2004 Yoarra
First edition 2004

Design: Henk Kemperman
Photography: Pieter van Houten, Yoarra
Illustrations: Yoarra

This book is published by: Purple Rhino Promotions.

email: sales@purplerhino.co.uk

Scoubidou strands are plastic hollow strands in beautiful colours.
With these strands you can knot fantastic keychains, hair clips
and also make animal figures out of them.
In this book I will teach you the basics you need to know
to start you knotting with Scoubidou strands.
We have made this book to let everyone enjoy this wonderful,
creative, and may I say addictive playmaterial by learning
the Scoubidou knotting
technique.
We would like to warn you,
once you start working
with the Scoubidou strands,
you won't be able to stop !

We hope you will enjoy
making the designs in this
book with the Scoubidou
strands as much as we have
enjoyed making this book.

Have lots of Scoubidou Fun !
Yoarra
&
Purple Rhino Promotions

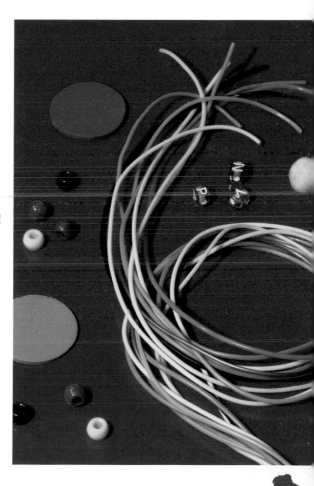

BEGINNING AND ENDING

Start with a knot/loop
Tie a Scoubidou strand with a semi knot around a pen or pencil
(see picture 1).
Then place a Scoubidou strand under the knot (see picture 2).
Now you make a straight or round knot (page 4-5, 6-7).

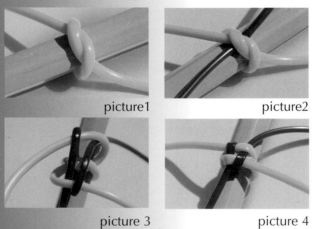

picture1   picture2

picture 3   picture 4

Start without a knot
To begin without a loop, take 2 strands and cross them over each other.
Using 1 strand make a semi knot in the middle of the other strand, so
all ends are even. Now you can start knotting, without having a loop.

Ending
If you have knotted with Scoubidou strands and you want to know how
to end (fasten off), then do the following: tie the last 2 knots a
little tighter and then you can continue to cut the Scoubidou strands
short. The Scoubidou strands will not come off anymore because they
are knotted.

All hand-knotted works are fastened this way. The keychain that you
can use daily, the animals that you can play with, but also the chains
with all the hand-knotted works Scoubidou strands are all cut short.

It's nice to use a plastic glue if you prefer to fasten them, which will then fix the short ends of the Scoubidou strands.

Of course you can also let the ends hang down and tie the strands together, and you can even put nice beads on them. This will make Scoubidou even prettier!

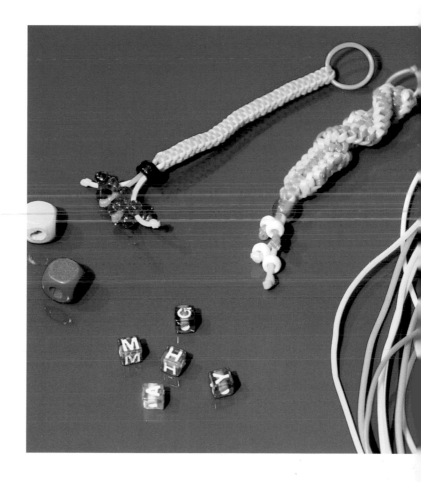

BASIC STRAIGHT KNOT

The knotting technique with 4 straight ends. You can start with or without a loop. (page 4)

To knot straight we make loops with the strands directly to the other sides of your knot.
With strand 1 make a loop towards the front side of the knot and with strand 2 make a loop towards the back of the knot.(see schedule 2)
Strand 4 goes over the open end of strand 2 through the loop of strand 1. With strand 3 you go over the open end of strand 1 and through the loop of strand 2. (see schedule 3)

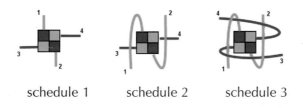

schedule 1   schedule 2   schedule 3

Tighten the strands nice and evenly and the first knot is ready.

Continue making loops this way.

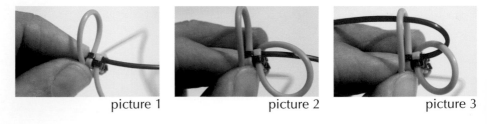

picture 1   picture 2   picture 3

If you continue knotting like this you will get a nice square knotted Scoubidou.

picture 4

picture 5

picture 6

BASIC ROUND KNOT

This knotting technique uses 2 Scoubidou strands
You can start with or without a loop (page 4).

To make a round knot you must make the loops using the 2 strands
diagonally opposite each other.

With the 4 strands make a diagonal loop down from right to left,
so that strand 4 is on the other side of strand 3. With strand 3 make
a loop diagonally up from left to the right, so that strand 3 is on
the other side of strand 4.

Pass strand 1 over the open end of strand 3 and through the loop of
strand 4. With strand 2 go over the open end of strand 4 passing
through the loop of strand 3.

Now tighten the strands evenly and a square will appear (see
picture 5).

Keep continuing knotting this way and a nice knotted Scoubidou will
appear.

schedule 1

schedule 2

schedule 3

picture 1

picture 2

picture 3

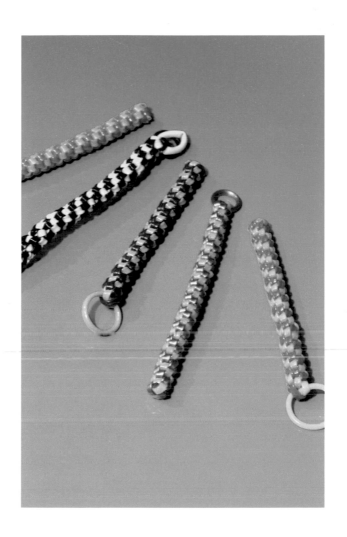

picture 4

picture 5

picture 6

BASIC STRAIGHT KNOT WITH SIX OR MORE STRANDS

With 3 straight knotted strands (six ends) you will get a nice straight knotted piece of work. If you knot with six ends, you have to arrange them so that you hold the knots nicely in order and follow the schedule well! Look at the schedule and pictures to see what is meant.
If you knot with more, then it should be more than 6 strands. Your piece of work gets wider, as you can see by the pictures. The schedule is for six ends, but you can also extend these to eight, ten or even more.

Begin with a loop or without a loop (page 4).

You make loops of the 4 opposite ones, in this case the light green and yellow strands.
With the light green strand 1 you make a loop straight up. With the light green strand 2 you make a loop straight down (this is just the same as the straight knot with four ends).

Now continue with the yellow strands, here do exactly the same. With the yellow strand 3 make a loop straight up. With the yellow strand 4 you make a loop straight down (see schedule 2).

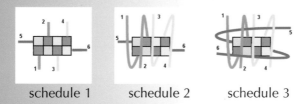

schedule 1   schedule 2   schedule 3

Now put the dark green strands to the left and right, only now through both loops. Pull the dark green strand 5 over the light green end of strand 1 and through the light green loop 2. Then the dark green strand 5 goes over the yellow end of strand 3 and then through the loop of the yellow strand 4.
With the dark green strand 6 go over the end of the yellow strand 4 through the yellow loop of strand 3. Then the dark green strand 6 goes over the end of the light green strand 2 and through the light green loop of strand 1 (see schedule 3).

Tie the knots nicely and continue with the next knot.

11

BASIC ROUND KNOT WITH SIX OR MORE STRANDS

With 3 round knotted strands (six ends) you will get a nice effect. With 6 knotted ends you have to be sure to hold the strands nicely in order to follow the schedule well! Look carefully at the schedule and pictures to see what is meant.

For ways to start please see the beginning (page 4).

Make loops of the 4 opposite strands, in this case the pink and blue Scoubidou strands. With the pink strand 1 make a loop diagonally down, so that strand 1 is on the other side of the pink strand 2. With the pink strand 2 make a loop diagonally up, so that the pink strand 2 is on the other side of strand 1 (this is just like the round knot with four ends).

Now continue with the blue strand 3 you will make a loop diagonally down so that strand 3 is on the other side of blue strand 4. With blue strand 4 make a diagonal loop so that blue strand 4 is on the other side of strand 3 (see schedule 2).

Pull strand 5 over the blue end of strand 4 and through the blue loop of 3. Then the red strand 5 goes over the pink end of the pink strand 2, and then through the loop of the pink strand 1. With the red strand 6 go over the end of the pink strand 1, through the pink loop of the pink strand 2. Then the red strand 6 goes over the end of the blue strand 3 and then through the loop of blue strand 4 (see schedule 3).

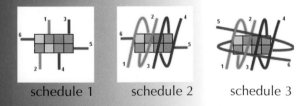

schedule 1   schedule 2   schedule 3

Continue knotting this way and a nice round knotted Scoubidou will appear.

COMBINATION STRAIGHT AND ROUND KNOT

You can use the round and straight technique nicely together, which will give a nice effect and nice pendants.

If you make a square Scoubidou and after 10 knots make 2 round knots, colors will change and cubes will appear.
Of course you can also make more round knots and then you will also get nice combinations.

Also, if you knot with more Scoubidou strands, a combination of round with straight will be very pretty, just look at the nice pendants below.

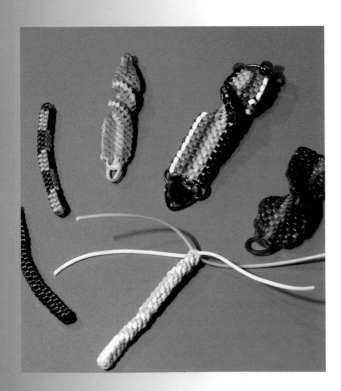

EXTENDING AND REDUCING STRANDS

Sometimes a strand is too short while you knot and you can't continue, below I will explain how you can add a Scoubidou strand while you are knotting.

You begin with two strands with a loop in the same colors.
Make a knot but don't pull it too tight (picture 1). Place under this knot the strand that you want to add (picture 2). Then pull the strand tight. Now the strand is added. Watch that you knot every other loop, like with the round or straight knots with six or more ends.

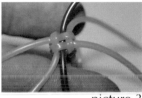

picture 1   picture 2   picture 3

Reducing strands
Sometimes you have to reduce strands. This works if you pull the two knots tight and to cut the desired strand short. Pull the next knot tight.

picture 4

BEADS AND BASIC KNOT WITH THREE STRANDS

You can also make nice pendants with beads. There are all kinds of many nice beads for sale in all kinds of sizes.

How you make the pendants depends on how you use the beads. Some beads are big enough to have 4 strands to be pulled through them and through some are beads only one strand will fit. Sometimes it's also nice to lay strands around the beads, like with the blue bracelet and the pink square bead on the black Scoubidou keychain.

Blue keychain
Also with more strands it can be nice to add beads, the blue keychain with name, which is made of 5 Scoubidou strands that are used in duplicate (double). Begin with a loop and make five straight knots, then divide the strands in 4 – 2 – 4 with the 4 strands on both sides you knot a straight Scoubidou and on the 2 middle strands you put the beads. After you have added the beads you make a knot with all strands.

Straight Knot with three strands/ends
Round with 3 ends:
Put the blue strand 1 over the purple strand 2.
Then you pass the purple strand 2 over the orange strand 3.
Then with the orange strand 3 go over the purple strand 2 and through the loop of the blue strand 1 (see schedule 2).

Now pull the strands even and a triangle will appear. You will get a round knot if you continue knotting this way.

schedule 1   schedule 2   schedule 3

Straight with three ends:
Follow steps 1 and 2.
With the next knot you need to put the loop to the left. Put the loops alternating right and left to create a straight knotted Scoubidou.

MACRAMÉ KNOT

You can also use the macramé (flat) or semi Macramé (turning) knots to create a nice flat bracelet or a nice turning keychain

Semi Macramé knot (turning)
Make a semi knot with the green strands around the black one so you get a loop (see picture 1). Then put the right green strand over the black strands (see picture 2).
Take the left green strand and put it over the other green strand (see picture 2). Place the green strand behind the black strands and through the loop of the green strand (see picture 3). Continue these step by step and your knot will turn around nicely.

Whole Macramé knot (flat)
To create the flat Macramé knot you first have to follow the steps/actions of the semi macramé knot as mentioned above. To make the Macramé knot flat we do the same knot with the other strand. You now put the left green strand over the black strand and the right strand over the green one (see picture 4) and then you pull this strand behind the black strands through the loop (see picture 5). Then you make the pictures 1 through 3 and then again the pictures 4 and 5, a nice flat knot will appear, very suitable for a bracelet!

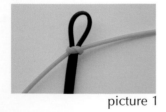
picture 1

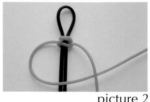
picture 2

picture 3

picture 4

picture 5

picture 6

ZIGZAG KNOT

You can create a zigzag pattern by making a round knot with the strands.
In theory you can make a zigzag with 2 strings (four ends), but also with more strands, the technique stays the same.

First you knot the two strands with the round knotting technique. You make for example eight round knots (it's up to you how many you choose).

Now you add the zigzag pattern. This you can do by knotting the other way. It's not difficult but you have to watch carefully, just look at the schedules of the pictures.

The first knot that you put after the round knot, is still a straight knot. Then you can follow the steps as mentioned below.
Put the black strand 1 diagonally up, so that strand 1 ends up on the left of black strand 2. Put the black strand 2 diagonally down, so that strand 2 ends up on the right side of strand 1.
Now pull yellow strand 3 over black strand 2 through the loop of black strand 1. The yellow strand 4 has to go over black strand 1 and through the loop of black strand 2.

You now have knotted the other way, make a few more knots to be able to see the effect well!

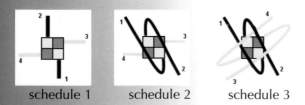

schedule 1   schedule 2   schedule 3

Make 8 zigzag knots and knot 8 normal ones…
This way you get a nice zigzag pattern.

Zigzag with 6 ends

You can knot with three Scoubidou strands to get a nice zigzag effect (then you will have six ends). Please look at the schedules carefully to see how you can make the zigzag knot.

Also here you have to make a straight knot in order continue knotting with the zigzag knotting schedule. Knotting with four or more Scoubidou strands goes the same way as knotting with three Scoubidou strands.

schedule 1   schedule 2   schedule 3

HELICOPTER AND BOTTLE TECHNIQUE

What's also nice and not difficult is to knot a helicopter...
You need to use 2 Scoubidou strands for this.

You start with Scoubidou strands with a loop (page 4). You knot about
5 cm straight (see picture 1). Now turn the knotted work upside down
and knot right back over the knotted part (see picture 1 and 2). This
method is mentioned below. This you do about 2 cm (see picture 2).

Now you face all strands up (see picture 4).
And carefully make a knot, make sure that this knot is nicely arranged
on top of the knotted part (see picture 5).
Now you make 2 straight knots.

The ends can be cut short at about 2 cm. Your helicopter is ready.

Bottle technique
You use the so-called bottle technique to be able to create a thickening
in the craft. This technique will be used to create a thickening in the
knotted strands, for example with the helicopter and the mouse. But it
can also be used to create a thickening part in a bracelet or other
crafts.

The bottle technique can be applied to the round knot (mouse spider).
But also to the straight knot (helicopter).

To be able to apply the bottle technique you have to turn your craft
around and knot around the knotted part (see picture 6).

picture 1

picture 2

picture 3

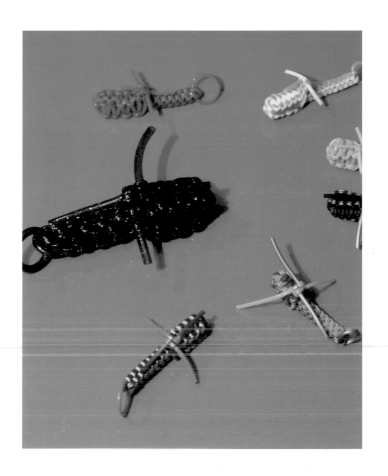

picture 4

picture 5

picture 6

FISH

To make this fish is very easy.
You knot the fish with 2 Scoubidou strands
It can be knotted round or straight. For this example we have chosen to
use the straight knot.

You start to knot with a loop. It doesn't matter if you knot straight or
round. Just choose yourself. Just knot about 8 cm.

Find a pencil and make the following knot around the pencil. Just
watch that the knot will stay nicely above the pencil. (see picture 1).
You can remove the pencil after you have made two knots, you will
then create an opening as you can see on picture 2. Now knot about
another 1.5 cm and pull the last two knots tighter and cut the ends
short.
Now take the ends with the loop and pull this one through the hole.
(see picture 3)

picture 1   picture 2   picture 3

Glue some nice eyes on to your fish and your fish is ready.

MOUSE

To make a cute mouse is not difficult to knot.
For this one you can use 3 strands, 2 grey ones and 1 pink strand.

Take a piece of pink strand of about 14 cm. Push a piece of flexible
wire through the strand. Now we start without a loop (page 4) around
the pink strand with wire (see picture 1). The pink strand with wire will
be the nose and the tail. Make sure the front of the pink strand will
stick out at about 1,5 cm in order to be able to bend the nose.
Knot about 4 knots.
Now take a piece of the pink scoubidou strand, about 7 cm, push wire
through this strand as well. Bend this like on picture 2. This will be the
ears. Add these ears now (see picture 3) and carefully make the next
knot, so that the ears will be fastened.

You now knot another 4 cm. (see picture). Now turn the knotted work
around and make a round knot back over the knotted part (see
picture 4). This method will be explained on page 22. Continue doing
this until the last knot will be around the pink strand.

Now bend with a pair of pliers a round nose in the 1.5 cm. Cut
anything away that's too long. You can bend the other end into a nice
tail. Glue eyes onto it and your mouse is ready.

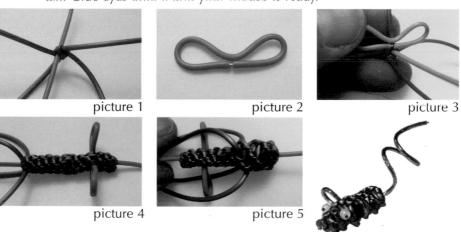

picture 1   picture 2   picture 3

picture 4   picture 5

FUNNY FACES

It's very nice to knot the faces, and not so difficult.
We knot a face with four strands. It can be knotted round or straight…

You make a big knot in the four Scoubidou strands (see picture 1).
It doesn't matter if you knot straight or round. Just choose yourself.
Knot about 15 cm and pull the big knot at the beginning out of it
(see picture 2).
Now knot both ends of your Scoubidou into an egg shape onto each
other (see picture 3). This can be done to make a bow with a piece of
Scoubidou. You can cut the ends not totally even at about 2 cm, which
will create a 'crew cut' (short hair).
Glue two eyes on it and your face is ready.
Knot in one of the hairs a loop to be able to hang them on to your
keychain.

Of course you can think of creating more things. You can stitch in the
'hairs' a piece of flexible wire, bend this with a cocktail stick till you
get curls (see picture 4).

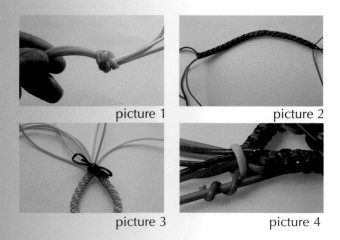

picture 1   picture 2

picture 3   picture 4

We can also make glasses, for this take a piece of Scoubidou. Push a piece of flexible wire into this strand. Wind this strand with the wire inside around a pencil (see picture 1). Repeat this another time (see picture 2). Now you have glasses (see picture 3).
Place it carefully on the face and bend the ends tight.

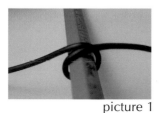  

picture 1   picture 2   picture 3

If you take 2 round pieces of foam, glue 2 eyes on them then you can glue this on the back of the glasses. A nose can be made by using a little pom pom!

HAIRCLIPS

Knot nice hairclips for yourself or friends, and have
a hairclip that no-one else has!
Great to give away as a gift!

At the craft stores you can buy the clip you need to
make the hairclip.
Or use an old clip, you can also knot around an alice
band or tiara.

You start without a loop with 4 strands. Make a semi knot around three
strands (see picture 1) and make the first knot with 8.
Now turn your craft around so that the squares lie on the outside. Now
knot straight with 8 until the desired length (this depends on the clip
size that you have).

Now you will glue the knotted strands on the clip. You have to hold
this well because the clip is a little round. Let it dry well after and you
will have a very nice clip for your hair!

You can also decorate the hairclip with the Macramé knot (see picture
3), but also try it with a tiara or alice band. Of course you can decorate
the Scoubidou strands with beads to make it even prettier.

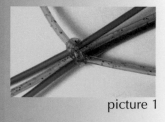

picture 1   picture 2   picture 3

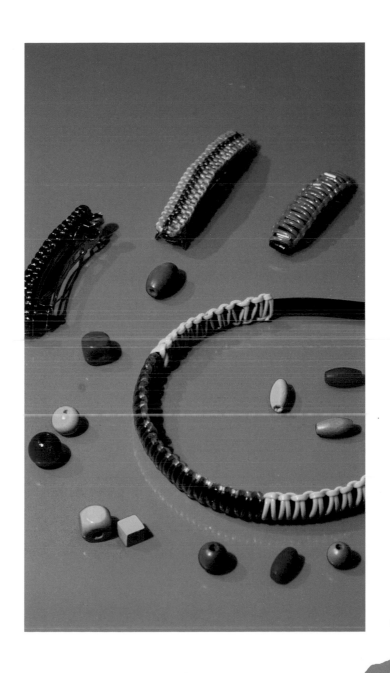

29

SNAKE

A nice knotting craft with Scoubidou strand is the Snake.
By putting flexible wire in the middle, you can bend the snake into all
kinds of shapes and you can also use this as a decoration for all kinds
of fun things. You will need 4 scoubidou strands and a short strand of
15 cm, a piece of flexible wire and two eyes.

You start with making a knot in the four strands (see picture 1).
Then you push the wire into the middle of the four strands and knot
around the wire with the round knot. Make plenty of knots. Then you
can remove the big knot, cut the wire and pull the last two knots tight
and cut the ends short (see picture 2). Now knot with the other side
around the wire till the strands that you are knotting with are about 15
cm long.

Now add another piece of Scoubidou strand, so we can knot with 6
ends. An explanation on how to add a strand can be seen on the page
'extending strands' with 8 knots (page 15). Now cut the wire short at
about 0.5 cm. Then place the red or pink Scoubidou strand around the
piece of wire (see picture 3). Cut the red or pink strands halfway,
so that a split/forked tongue will appear.

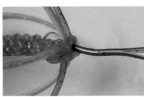

Now knot about another ten knots and cut the outside two
strands short, and make two more knots with four
strands.
Glue the eyes on the snake.

  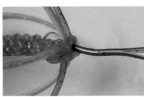

picture 1   picture 2   picture 3

KNOTTING A SPIDER

Shiver with this spider. This is fairly easy to make, only a little awkward because you have to work around the wires.
You use for this 3 black strands, 4 pieces of wire of about 15 cm and two wobbly eyes.

Take a black strand, cut about 4 pieces of about 15 cm. Push wire through the strands, this will be the legs. Now You begin without a loop. Knot 4 round knots.
Add 1 strand with wire (see picture 1). Now make 4 knots and add again a strand with wire.
Do this twice again and knot after the last leg 3 knots (see picture 2).

Now knot back around the knotted part (with the bottle technique). This you do carefully through the wires. Watch that you knot all the way through till the last knot will be a knot that is not around the knotted part, so that the square appears again. Cut the strands short.

Bend the legs around your finger till they are even (see picture 3). At the end of the legs, bend the ends. (see picture of the spider)
Now add the eyes and let everyone shiver at the spider!

picture 1

picture 2

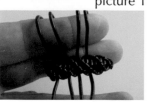

picture 3

Special thanks from Amanda Miles:
To my sisters Emily and Charlotte Miles
who without them it would not have
happened and to my Dad,
who gave me all the encouragement
and support.

Thank you !